Campanulas ir

Peter Lewis

All drawings, including the front cover, by David Milner
Edited and typeset by George Parker
Consultant editor to the Booklet Series: Tony Lord

© The Hardy Plant Society – November 2002

ISBN 0 901687 19 7

Campanula punctataa

Acknowledgements

FOR EVERY GENUS THERE IS NEED FOR LITERATURE that is within the reach of the serious gardener, both the relative novice and the more experienced. I hope this booklet, while not aimed at the botanically minded nor at the specialist campanula collector and grower, will be of help to those who love bellflowers and wish to grow them among other genera in their open garden.

"Whence comes the moss that builds up slowly on the roof?"

Having spent some thirty years "messing about with campanulas", I find it difficult either to credit or to blame others for their help; they have been too numerous to single out. How often one has picked up useful information from unknown folk while garden visiting, and their help has perhaps been as useful in the long run as doctrine assimilated from more formal contacts with plantsmen, nurserymen and botanists, be they ever so wise and experienced - and these have been many.

I owe as much as anything to contacts within the Cambridge University Botanic Garden, from directors to taxonomists to muddy-fingered weeders out on the beds and screes. Moreover, I am in the debt of Margaret Lynch, who has been a staunch and most patient colleague in former publications. But above all my debt to Susan, my wife, is inexpressibly more than is the invariable custom in acknowledgment lists. She broke me in to campanulas in the first place and she has an eye and feelings for plants so much better than I have. And, anyway, she could have made a better job of this booklet than I have done.

Introduction

VISUALLY A VERY SATISFYING SHAPE, the bell gives its name to the genus *Campanula*, derived from the late Latin (and modern Italian) word, *campana*; campanula can be interpreted as 'little bell'. The common names of most European languages echo the bell-shape: bellflower, cloche, and glocke among them.

Long known and grown, campanulas remain among the most popular of genera. Their diversity being so wide, most types of garden have a place for them - herbaceous borders, cottage gardens, alpine gardens, woodland gardens, container gardens, window boxes, hanging baskets, pots and even cutting gardens - there is a broad selection of forms and sizes for every situation and taste. They are so adaptable.

A number of campanulas native to Europe have been introduced into cultivation and selected and bred for garden value, while new cultivars and hybrids are continually being produced for plant lovers. North America has only a few endemic species and not many of them find a place in the general garden though there are one or two that specialised alpine growers will fight and die for. Asia, southern Africa, Australia and New Zealand have no campanulas; these are replaced by other genera of the family, notably *Wahlenbergia*, which only has one diminutive representative in Europe, including Britain

Existing literature on the genus is varied: complex and detailed floras are numerous and coverage is extensive. One of the more practical handbooks for gardeners (as well as botanists) is that of Clifford Crook, but this is now largely outdated. The more recent *Campanulas* (1989), sponsored by the Hardy Plant Society, and its 1998 revision are out of print and also need revising.

The present booklet deals with the more commonly grown species, cultivars and hybrids grown by keen gardeners, omitting the rarer and more difficult campanulas suited to experienced alpine and specialist growers and often grown in pots for display and competition.

As the genus originates in the temperate northern hemisphere, hardiness is rarely a problem unless a plant is inappropriately situated. Siting is not difficult as tolerance to sun, or relative lack of it, can usually be accommodated. Unlike their cousins, the lobelias, they are not toxic: the milky sap is harmless latex and in fact campanula leaves and roots have been, and are, used as food and medicine.

It has not often been pointed out or acknowledged that, as a general rule, the genus is not a long-lived one and this is usually why so many of the tempting cultivars recorded in past nursery catalogues leave no trace. It is also the explanation for their abundant, and sometimes unpopular capacity for seeding and running, which are in fact understandable survival mechanisms. It is either our fortune or misfortune that the spreading by seeding very rarely gives plants true to type. Thus a poor specimen is quite liable to produce a new or attractive offspring; the wise and optimistic plantsman leaves a selection of seedlings in hopefulness. Those of us who do not boast of such wisdom or optimism have to be thankful for such as Maurice Prichard and Alan Bloom who have shown these enviable virtues and given us some of our most valued selections.

Campanula carpatica

Campanulas: Some Facts & Figures

A VERY BRIEF HISTORY

It is not known how long campanulas have been grown, either as food or as vegetables, but we do know when some of them were brought into cultivation as garden flowers. Prior to this they were known in the herb gardens of the old monasteries of Britain and Europe as medicine for sore throats and the like - hence the 'Throatwort', *C. trachelium*. The status of some is uncertain: *Campanula rapunculus*, the rampion of the brothers Grimm, may well have been grown in monastery gardens and elsewhere for its edible white root until overtaken by its rival, the carrot, which had a more attractive colour and yielded itself more readily to the breeder.

Campanulas figure in the old floras such as Miller's and Gerard's, and, in addition to the endemic species, which also provide some popular cultivars, were certainly imported into Britain from the Continent as early as the 1590s.

There have been notable plant-hunters who have introduced both preserved and living plant material to Kew and other botanic gardens; such are Sibthorp and von Bieberstein working in the Caucasus, Fischer in Russia and Siberia, and others working in Turkey and the Middle East.

Some famous botanists, such as the de Candolles and Boissier, as well as early gardening personalities like Correvon in Switzerland, Reginald Farrer, E. A. Bowles, the Ingwersens and Margery Fish in Britain, and Liberty Hyde Bailey in the USA, have devoted much attention to campanulas, leaving a great deal of both authoritative and discursive literature at our command, and the genus figured frequently in literature such as the *Gardeners' Chronicle*. More recently, well-known nurserymen such as Maurice Prichard, Clarence Elliott and Alan Bloom have both imported and introduced species and cultivars that are still in cultivation, and some modern plant-hunters have introduced especially alpine species from the mountains of Europe, Asia and the Himalayas.

Not least among its claims to fame, the harebell is adopted as the flower of the region of Sweden where Linnaeus worked at Uppsala.

GEOGRAPHY

Campanulas are confined to the northern hemisphere and virtually all are native to areas north of the Tropic of Cancer; the one, or perhaps two, being found just south of this in the Highlands of Ethiopia and Kenya are closely related to Mediterranean species. It might be said that the centre of diversity is the Mediterranean region, especially in the mountains and higher altitudes, with spread to the north and east particularly: to Scandinavia, Caucasus, the Middle East and as far as Siberia and Himalaya. In a broad sense the family *Campanulaceae* is replaced in the southern hemisphere with *Wahlenbergia* and in the equatorial regions with *Lobelia*.

The Americas are poor in *Campanula*, the few natives being confined to the North. The harebell, which, in one or other of its forms, grows up to the far north of every continent, is found down the main mountain chains as far as New Mexico. Apart from two or three rare alpines in the mountains, further south the biennial *C. americana* is the only native that finds a place in gardens though several species of European origin have been introduced and become well naturalised.

While distribution tends toward higher elevations, the lowland species are widely scattered, and the fact that they have frequently and easily naturalised from garden escapes is a sign of the flexibility they offer in cultivation.

Most of the well-known garden campanulas are widely distributed in their native habitats, often with distinct regional variations within the species. This, and the fact that some are variable within their narrow endemic region, is the origin of many of our subspecies and cultivars, quite apart from variations from breeding in cultivation. A good principle to adopt in cultivation, with this or any other genus, is a readiness to simulate natural conditions in the garden as far as is practicable.

The common factor running through the whole genus is a strong preference for rapid drainage and a tendency toward alkaline soils; the few exceptions are easily accommodated.

Britain has a handful of native campanulas, apart from introductions of such antiquity that their exact standing has sometimes been queried. In more recent years others have escaped from gardens and become naturalised in such places as abandoned railway cuttings where some, far from their native land, have even acquired vernacular names.

BOTANY

Apart from one or two short-lived or monocarpic plants and a few biennials, most of the campanulas described here are hardy perennials. They are leafy-stemmed plants arising from either tuberous or fine, running roots with a basal rosette whose leaves are often different from the stem-leaves. These basal leaves are frequently withered away when the plant is in bud and flower. Hence the anomaly of *Campanula rotundifolia* - the round-leaved bellflower, alias the harebell, which has more or less needle-shaped stem-leaves. The round leaves of 'rotundifolia' have, of course withered and perished by the time the plant is in flower.

Most of the larger species are deciduous. Some of the smaller alpines keep their green rosette through the onslaughts of winter but, provided that they are planted in really well drained spots in the garden, are very hardy and will flourish for many years.

Stem-leaves are alternate and generally reduce in size up the stem, while the petioles or leaf-stems, if present, become shorter. There are frequently buds in the leaf-axils that can develop into side-shoots if the main stem is damaged and advantage is taken of this to produce a second flowering after the main one is over.

The flowers are relatively simple, regular, bisexual, and their parts normally in fives. The five petals of the corolla are fused at their base, where the five free stamens are inserted. The style, connecting the inferior ovary to the stigma, is generally divided into three, occasionally five, with the ovary divided to match. The seed capsule splits by pores when the seed is ripe and this seed is often very fine. This ripened capsule, either upright or pendent, always has the pores at the upper end so that shaking in the wind tends to scatter seed some distance from the mother plant. The calyx is five-parted and may be erect or more or less reflexed and often has appendages between the sepals.

A characteristic of the genus and the family is that the pollen-bearing stamens have withered away at the time of flowering, having deposited their pollen on the style of their own flower. Pollination is by bees or hover-flies which, in seeking the nectar found at the base of the anthers, brush against the style, pick up the pollen and subsequently transfer this to the stigmas on their entry into another flower. If by any chance the flower remains unpollinated, the stigmas will curl round and touch their own style, picking up their own pollen and thus self-pollinating. This is but a fail-safe mechanism as last resort. Cross-pollination is always preferred and, indeed, usually takes place. Early- or unusually late-flowering more often leads to self-pollination, when weather is too cool or dull for insects to be flying, though hover-flies are more adaptable in this respect.

Campanulas have no perfume and butterflies, moths etc show little interest, nor does their build encourage penetration of the bell-flower; this said, the smell of the nectar must be enough to attract bees, especially bumble bees. One campanula, *C. versicolor*, is said to have a clove perfume, detected however only by those with a very fine sense of smell.

Root systems vary from species to species: some have a simple taproot; some, like *C. lactiflora*, a thick fleshy rootstock, often much branched and contorted with age and becoming woody; whilst others, like *C. rapunculoides* have fine, running white rhizomes reminiscent of couch grass.

Growth starts in early to late spring and is rapid up to the flowering period in early to late summer. After flowering the stem and leaves die back but there may be considerable growth at the root system and basal rosette, making autumn a favourable time for propagation by division. Nursery propagators take advantage of this to take offshoots and cuttings before winter dormancy.

This is the place to point out the differences between three closely related genera, *Campanula*, *Symphyandra* and *Adenophora*, as they are frequently confused in the trade and in gardens. *Adenophora* frequently masquerades as *Campanula*, and vice-versa. With discretion, the following test can be applied before acquiring a plant: if the flower is carefully stripped of petals, it will be seen that in *Campanula* the style arises from the ovary with the five free stamens, usually withered by the time the flower has opened. In *Symphyandra* the stamens are fused into a tube round the style. In *Adenophora* the style arises from a small disc that surrounds its base; this may be between 1mm and 8mm in height, depending on species. These are the characteristics by which botanists have separated the three genera, aside from their different regions of origin.

Cultivation

MOST OF THE SPECIES with which we are concerned are easily-grown plants which readily adapt to most reasonable garden conditions but the best and longest-lived plants will be those that are given habitat, environment and soil conditions that simulate their growing situation in the wild as closely as possible. It is no unusual thing to ask for good drainage and, in most cases, a fairly sunny position, to have them give of their best and, given these, soil type is not of cardinal importance. While many tend to prefer slightly alkaline conditions, the exceptions are more frequently found among the alpines. Where pH is of some significance it will be pointed out under the species concerned.

The tall, erect-growing species, making good subjects for the back of the border, will thrive on the well-cultivated soil which all such plants like. They mostly appreciate sun and moisture-holding yet well-drained situations (and these are not contradictory). Heavy clay needs modification with humus and perhaps added grit or sand; this is difficult on a large scale, perhaps, but should be kept in mind. Staking may be needed in exposed positions as wind can be hard on them but this is not difficult to conceal if necessary. Some of these taller species are rather intolerant of drought, which makes for brittleness in the stem but, again, adequate humus in the soil takes care of this.

Very few need feeding, which may only soften them with ensuing soft growth rather than stiff stems and abundant flowers. Amongst the few is *C. persicifolia*, short-lived on the mountains from which it comes and dependent on frequent renewal. It will appreciate tender loving care and this means some feeding but, above all, careful moving and propagation every year or two - and this is especially true of the double cultivars. Dead-heading is rewarding here.

However, while dead-heading is more than tedious in most, the taller species and cultivars can be encouraged to give a second blooming by cutting back their stems after the first flush of flowers; subsequent side-stems can fully recompense this attention. This is especially true of *C. lactiflora* in all colours, which should only be cut back to the side-stems which show at this time, for it is they that will provide the new flowers. *C. latifolia*, *C. latiloba* and *C. trachelium* are a little less successful in this respect and should be cut back to a lower point of the stem (while leaving some feeding leaves); if they do not respond, at least one has tidied the border, for the dead flowers are unkempt at best. Of course, if seed is needed this must mean leaving the flowers to mature.

While these last three are among those that naturally grow at woodland edge and in hedgerow, they will tolerate sunny positions as well, although perhaps with a shorter flowering period, so long as they do not dry out too much. They make, of course, excellent woodland garden subjects.

While many campanulas will tolerate pot culture, provided they are suitably cared for, drying out will soon ruin their attractiveness. These days of buying pot-cultured specimens, one is tempted to enjoy the flowering before planting out but the compost, or apology for it, in which the plant is sold should be taken into account, for it will not suffice the plant for long, especially as it is probably already pot-bound. Daily watering (the emphasis is on daily) may take care of it very temporarily; if it is to be grown in a larger container it is best moved and given a better growing medium without delay. Large containers are little different from open soil but the smaller need constant care, as do window-boxes that are ideal for the smaller subjects, which make a change from the summer pansies, though they will not last so long in flower. The fashionable hanging basket is suitable for the *C. poscharskyana* hybrids, which can flower most of the summer if cut back as flowers fade. Here they may be grown either on their own or in combination with other traditional denizens of the basket. Those who indulge in such will not need the reminder about watering, though baskets with a bottom reservoir are less of a chore.

Of the rock garden little need be said as there is probably good drainage there anyway. All the smaller campanulas are thoroughly at home there and will thrive.

Propagation

SEED

FEW CAMPANULAS ARE AVAILABLE AS SEED from commercial seedsmen so the main source must be the specialist garden societies, whose annual seed lists invariably offer a wide selection. Some specialist seedsmen and nurseries may also have seed available. Seed-hunting expeditions, usually by botanists and dedicated plant-hunters, can be very useful; these usually will also be found through the specialist societies, especially the alpine ones. The least reliable but frequently the most interesting, if somewhat unpredictable, source is the gardens of friends.

By their very nature campanulas are easy from seed. Sowing is best done in late autumn through to late winter. This is usually and most conveniently done in pots of well-drained compost that can subsequently be left exposed to winter weather. Most seed is fine; it should be sown on the surface of the compost and then covered very lightly with horticultural grit or very sharp sand. It is important to know that light is necessary for germination in this genus. Everyone will have their favourite sowing medium: a mixture of soil-based compost with added grit makes a good seedbed, John Innes No.1 being probably the favourite but the devil you know is usually the safest. Virtually all species will benefit from actual freezing to assist germination, which is often very quick. If sowing is done carefully and thinly, germinated seedlings can be potted forward at an early stage but little is lost if some growth is made before transplanting, again if seed is sown thinly, ensuring minimal damage to roots. Moving to larger pots, with some protection at early stages, will ensure strong plant growth ready for planting out *in situ* in spring. There is little benefit in early feeding, which will give weak, fleshy, leafy growth at the expense of the healthy vigour natural to the genus. Indeed, with rare exceptions, feeding campanulas is a superfluous activity.

Campanula seed will keep in packets in a refrigerator, preferably with silica gel alongside, for a number of years and retain a high rate of germination.

CUTTINGS AND DIVISION

Most species may be propagated by either of these two means, and of course, they are the only ways of keeping cultivars true.

Taking cuttings is not a difficult task, given suitable timing and some care and attention. As with any genus, the best time is while there is vigorous growth and this is most likely to be early spring or indeed autumn when the plant is consolidating itself, foliage perhaps cut back to help it. The latter is the preferred time for the nurseryman as he wants to have saleable plants for the next season. Many species will produce offsets or 'Irishman's cuttings', and these are certainly the easiest to manage. At almost any time of the year but again especially in spring and autumn, side stems may be cut cleanly close to the rootstock and, with or without hormone (but if used it is preferable for this to be in powder form), these may be inserted in a propagating compost, which should be largely grit and sharp sand, in trays or individual pots; these may be carefully watered and covered with translucent plastic. Extra heat is not generally necessary but the cuttings should not be allowed to chill: an unheated greenhouse will suffice.

Where there is a large rootstock - often a massive, gnarled affair as in the case of C. *lactiflora* and others - this may literally be chopped into several pieces, the older centre discarded, and where possible clean outer pieces with some fresh fibrous material taken and replanted in a favourable compost or even warm open ground. This is a time when sogginess must be avoided. For most, potting up for a later replanting will be the wisest course as control of moisture, temperature and exposure are then more easily controlled.

Numerous species are already runners and the roots are easily severed between nodes and each leaf-rosette replanted, its own root sections already active. Incidentally, this is also a modest means of restraining these species; unseen and unnoticed root pieces will be enough to maintain their running habit!

Pests & Diseases

CAMPANULAS SUFFER FROM FEW PROBLEMS of either pest or disease specific to the genus and those which do affect them are likely to be common to other plants in the garden.

One of the commonest problems, especially in the wetter areas and seasons, is the slug and to a lesser extent, in pots especially, the snail. Various remedies are offered: cinders, sawdust, grit, tapes and 'slug pubs' among them. While none is likely to be 100% effective, they are deterrents and can be useful in some situations. Although campanulas seem to be especially attractive to these pests the latter are a garden problem to which the only certain answer is a biological deterrent, the sowing in the soil of nematodes that are parasitic on slug and snail. In any case, wet and inadequately drained soils are likely to harbour more menacing populations and the tackling of drainage deficiencies is always a good initiative. The better-drained soils, while being rich and moisture-retentive, will give a stronger, more robust plant that will resist pest attacks.

Aphids rarely trouble campanulas even when they are abundant on neighbouring plants. Rabbits are partial to campanulas but fencing is the only answer to this problem - or a free-range dog!

Rusts have been experienced, especially on the vulnerable *C. persicifolia*. The campanula rust, *Puccinia campanulae*, fulfills its entire life cycle on campanula species (or *Jasione montana*). Another rust alternates its life cycle between campanula species and *Pinus sylvestris*, the Scots Pine, but it is not common and an individual choice has to be made here! Damp, inadequately ventilated corners and over-fertilised and weak growth favour this problem and the best deterrent available rests in good culture methods and avoidance of excessive, or even any, nitrogenous fertiliser. A vigorously growing plant is far less vulnerable to rusts. However, it may be that a recently acquired plant shows warning signs of small orange pustules on the underside of leaves or even stems; these may be followed by blotches on the upper side of leaves and defoliation of the plant if neglected. Proprietary fungicides may be considered the treatment of choice but cutting back stems to ground level can result in renewed, fresh, clean growth.

Plant Associations

GIVEN THAT THE NORMAL BLUE of campanulas in fact contains a red factor all too obvious to photographic emulsion but considerably less so to the human eye, they are adaptable in their associations and generally combine well with reds. Red roses under-planted with campanulas are an old favourite. But it is only necessary to place a bright lilac-blue campanula alongside a gentian or delphinium, to name but two, to see the offending red factor at its most belligerent.

Campanulas, whatever their size and spread, have always been cottage garden favourites and it is in such that they perhaps seem most natural. Here they will seldom appear out of place in virtually any combination where riotous living is the natural order.

The taller species and their cultivars fit well into the herbaceous border, especially the *C. lactiflora* in its variants at the back; bold plantings of these, especially 'Loddon Anna' are always impressive, and *Knautia macedonica* at its feet with pink lavender in the foreground makes a beautiful combination which can be seen in some of the larger gardens such as Hidcote and the neighbouring Kiftsgate. *C. latiloba* can be effective here also, but the unsubtle shades of 'Highcliffe' and 'Percy Piper', very similar, are less adaptable than 'Hidcote Amethyst' Of course, the white variants of all will fit in without difficulty in any combination but especially in white gardens. *C. persicifolia* fits this slot also, but is especially good with some of the more awkward coloured roses, such as 'Zéphirine Drouhin'.

C. latifolia, being a plant of hedgerows and woodland edges, looks at home in woodland gardens, possibly along with *C. trachelium*; both can take fair shade and, planted beneath apples, cherries and plums, can help to reduce the formal look. In these situations they may also replace spring bulbs. *C. rapunculoides* will be happy here also - but it is best kept on its own in places where it cannot take over the whole show.

The smaller species such as *C. carpatica* make good edging plants for borders, again at best in small clumps; this species has a wide range of shades that make it adaptable. Care should be taken not to plant these close to edges where they will overrun grass and kill it. The still smaller species, which are often treated either as rock garden plants or otherwise exclusively as container or basket subjects, make excellent edging between the border and a gravel path, where better drainage is likely to be available. Among those that will last here for years are *C. poscharskyana* and hybrids, like 'Constellation' and 'E. K. Toogood', *C. portenschlagiana* and *C. garganica* subsp. *cephallenica.* Most of these blend well with the sturdier small pinks, where colour, height and environment preferences are shared.

Campanula persicifolia cup-and-saucer

Campanulas for Cutting & In

IN THE GARDEN THE FLOWERING PERIOD of many
is relatively short but they make very adaptable cut flowers   in the
house and distanced from their natural pollinators, last for much longer.
Advantage is taken of this in Scandinavian countries where indoor plants
are especially treasured: pot plants such as *C. formanekiana* have been
grown specifically for the house and remain in flower for months instead of
the week or two anticipated in the open garden. Some of the smaller species
and their cultivars are now imported into Britain and other countries - as
far distant as Japan and the USA, and are available in florists. They are
usually forced into early-season flowering when even their pollinators are
not flying and so they remain in flower, even in the open, and are very
acceptable at a time of year when flowers are few in the temperate North.

There was a day when *C. pyramidalis,* the chimney bellflower, was
grown as an enormous pot plant for the hall - or in the chimneybreast,
where it got its name. Fashion, as well as the lack of labour needed to
produce it, has removed it from this use but it can still make a stunning
show.

C. persicifolia and its cultivars are probably the only real florists' plants;
favourites on their own, in single colours, or with blue and white blooms
mixed. In mixed arrangements they combine well. *C. persicifolia* planted in
a good moist soil, probably as part of the vegetable garden, has been grown
specifically for cutting. Planted in double rows to give protection from wind
(though they might still need some staking) and to allow of easy access,
they will need dividing and moving every other year, but will provide the
cutting material which makes this well worth the trouble. The aim is to
grow, in a sunny, well-ventilated spot, healthy plants with strong stems and
to avoid possible risk of rust. They are best picked in the cool of the
morning or evening and the ends of the stems singed before plunging deep
in water for a long drink before using.

Other border campanulas of value for cutting are *C. glomerata,*
especially in its variants 'Dahurica' and 'Superba', *C. alliariifolia,* which
serves well in minimalist arrangements where its creamy-white arching
stems can be emphasised; the redder variants of *C. punctata* and *C.
takesimana,* especially 'Elizabeth' and the brilliant blue-violet hybrid 'Kent
Belle'.

The coarser species, like *C. trachelium,* offer little except in its double
cultivars, but *C. rapunculoides* can be most effective, probably on its own, in

vase, and the same applies to *C. latifolia*. Removal of some leaves will be necessary.

C. *lactiflora* in its more colourful variants like 'Loddon Anna' and 'Prichard's Variety' come into their own, in large arrangements, especially when used on their own. If these are planted in the border in the large clumps that make them most imposing, a few bold stems thinned from such clumps provide good indoor material.

Sprays of the smaller campanulas such as *C. portenschlagiana* and *C. poscharskyana* are ideal in cottage posy bowls where usually the kaleidoscope of colours fails to hinder the campanulas from mixing with the true blues that otherwise offend and they are so floriferous that stems removed will not be noticed - indeed, they are soon replaced. *C. carpatica* can be treated the same but the size of flower on short stems can make them a little clumsy.

Bearing in mind that, once cut and carefully handled, the flowers will last longer inside than left in the open garden, most are worth trying! The bonus will also be repeat flowering as autumn approaches.

Campanula portenschlagiana

18

Campanulas: an alphabetical listing

C. alliariifolia
Found in Turkey and the Caucasus. This forms a stout perennial root, usually deeply fanged. The basal rosette is of large, somewhat coarse shield-shaped leaves on petioles longer than the blade. They are felted above and quite woolly beneath. Several arching stems arise from the basal rosette. The main stems bear short unilateral erect pedicels bearing cream or white pendent narrow bellflowers with slightly reflexed petals. In the wild there are purplish-white flower forms but in cultivation only white to cream flowers are seen. This is an easy but coarse plant for the wild garden, though the stems can be used for cut flowers. Z3

C. barbata
European Alps, mostly on higher acidic meadows, also SW Poland and one small area of Norway. This is a biennial or short-lived perennial. The stolon or deep taproot produces a tuft of lanceolate leaves and one or several stems that bear a few strap-shaped leaves and one or a few pendent pale lavender-blue flowers. The petals are divided to one-third and slightly reflexed to reveal the beard at the tips and within. Height is 20-30cm. Z6

C.b. var. alba
The white variety, which appears to be commoner in cultivation than in the wild.

C. bononiensis
Widespread in Central and Eastern Europe. This is a greyish plant to 80cm with a basal rosette of stalked heart-shaped leaves and a stem bearing similar but stalkless leaves growing shorter towards the tip and which partially clasp the stem at leaf axils. There is a long spike of smallish funnel-shaped pendent flowers. The plant is glabrous, the flowers relatively small and unspectacular, and a wild garden is its most suitable habitat. It is either biennial or a short-lived perennial. Z3

C. 'Burghaltii' AGM
An old garden hybrid of unrecorded origin between C. punctata and C. latifolia, the former being the seed parent, the latter providing the pollen. The basal leaves are heart-shaped on stalks as long as the leaf-blades and slightly winged. The leaves become progressively more oval at their base but more pointed up the stem, with shortening stalks. The upper surface of the leaf is smooth but there are short hairs on the veins of the underside and also on the stems. These are somewhat branched and flowers are borne

terminally in the leaf-axils. These are very dark amethyst-purple in bud and pearly dove-grey or lilac, slightly hairy within and darkening to a true blue as they die. The style is tripartite. No seed is set so division in spring or rooting fresh spring growths from the rootstock are effective means of propagation. The plant has a slightly running root system but is not as vigorous as the *punctata* parent, and it does not appear to be a long-lived plant. Frequent division and replanting will keep the plant going; it is happier in a shady and/or moist soil, or at least one that does not dry out, and a lighter one for preference. Z7

C. carpatica AGM

Comes from the Carpathian mountains, where it is very variable, and proves hardy and equally diverse in cultivation. It has produced many named variants, popular in gardens for many years and versatile in that, while they are of alpine dimensions, they can be grown with little trouble in most garden situations where good drainage is provided. From a perennial rootstock basal rosettes of bright green roundish leaves wither as the stems grow and bear oval to triangular leaves on petioles which diminish up the stem while the leaves become more heart-shaped. With a height of 15-30cm, open upward-facing sun-seeking flowers are of many shades and shapes. This is a long-lived species and can be long-lasting over a season if, as the flowers fade it is given a haircut to stimulate new buds and further flowerings, possibly from May to September in some of the more vigorous cases. Many cultivars have been named over the years, and new ones continue to be produced. Naming is a minefield. Z3

C.c. forma *alba*

Pale green stems and leaves. White flowers, fairly flat. 25cm

C.c. f. *a.* 'Bressingham White'

Introduced by Blooms of Bressingham. To 20cm high, spread 35cm Compact and erect. Leaves 3.2cm long x 2cm medium dark green, hairy. Calyx hairy, tinted burgundy. Flower stems 12cm. Flowers 3-4cm diameter x 3cm, bell-shaped, erect, white with deep blue trace at centre. Flowering from June.

C.c. f. *a.* 'Snowdrift'

Bears medium-sized flowers of a very pure white on a slow-growing, compact plant.

C.c. f. *a.* 'Weisse Clips' (White Clips)

From Germany. A vigorous pure white that is also supposed to come true from seed, in which form it is frequently offered.

C.c. 'Bees' Variety'

Flowers deepest purple. To 15cm. The true plant is probably extinct.

C.c. 'Blaue Clips' (Blue Clips)
From Germany. Hairy, grass-green leaves in a low mound, 20cm x 1.5cm. Calyx lighter green than stems, tinged burgundy. Flower stems 8cm, tinged burgundy, hairy. Flowers 4.5cm wide x 3.5cm deep, cup-shaped, mid-violet, darker without, veined lighter lilac. Has been said to come true from seed.

C.c. 'Blue Ball'
A somewhat unreliable double blue, producing at first some single flowers. It is compact, about 10-15cm tall. The doubling seems dependent on high exposure to sunlight.

C.c. 'Blue Moonlight'
An old cultivar from Alan Bloom. Forms a compact clump 20-30cm. Leaves 2 x 1.5cm grass-green, few hairs upper surface, more beneath. Calyx tinged burgundy. Flower stems 9cm. Flowers 5.5cm, open saucers, light violet, fading to violet blue, giving impression of blue and white shading, dark purple trace outside.

C.c. 'Caerulea'
A compact plant with very pale sky blue flowers.

C.c. 'Carillon'
Flowers intermediate shade, more blue than any. Flowers mostly flat, losing bell shape. Height 20cm.

C.c. 'Chewton Joy'
A dwarf, compact variety bearing medium-sized flowers of a pale opaque blue fading toward the centre, free and late flowering. 20cm.

C.c. 'Claribel'
Similar to the better-known but later-flowering 'Chewton Joy'; light violet-blue, wide-cupped flowers 3cm across, paling toward the centre. 10-15cm.

C.c. 'China Cup'
Stems 10-15cm. Flower an upstanding pale blue open cup, 5cm across, reflexed margins.

C.c. 'Convexity'
Height to 30cm, medium green spreading leaves, flowers 5cm across, saucer-shaped on long stems, bright violet-blue with distinct veins.

C.c. 'Craven Bells'
Introduced by Reginald Farrer. An old selection has china blue flowers of very round shape.

C.c. 'Ditton Blue'
Low mound to 15cm. Leaves 2.5 x 2cm, grass-green, hairy. Calyx tinged burgundy, upper surface speckled wine. Flower stems 10cm, hairy. Flowers

4.5cm across, 2.5cm deep, good upright bell-shape, bright purple with paler lavender veining outside corolla.

C.c. 'Far Forest'
Height to 25cm. Width 30-40cm, medium green leaves. Flower stems 18cm. Flowers bell-shaped, small, 1.7cm across, 2.5cm deep, very freely produced, white, slightly flushed and finely edged pale lavender, deep violet-blue at centre and reverse. Distinctive and late flowering. The original clone is probably extinct.

C.c. 'Georg Arends'
Has rich violet blue flowers

C.c. 'Glacier Blanc'
Flowers large, silvery-white tinged blue; more wide-open than 'Weisse Clips', long-flowering from April-October.

C.c. 'Glacier Bleu'
Numerous large violet-blue flowers on stems 25-40cm, May-October.

C.c. 'Glacier Ultra'
Tall stems 30-40cm. Flowers violet, more wide-open than 'Kobaltglocke'. Flowering April-October.

C.c. 'Harvest Moon'
Introduced by Maurice Prichard. Flowers forming large, flat saucer, described as a pale 'Riverslea'.

C.c. 'Karpatenkrone'
Mid-blue with a wide-open flower.

C.c. 'Kathy'
Medium sized flowers of pale shaded blue, close to 'Caerulea'.

C.c. 'Kobaltglocke'
Flower colour is deep violet

C.c. 'Lavender'
Of the palest lavender blue.

C.c. 'Mattock's Double'
Wide blue double flowers.

C.c. 'Maureen Haddon'
Named after one of the staff of Bloom's of Bressingham. Compact, with light green leaves and petite flowers of mid blue. It is less vigorous than some.

C.c. 'Moonlight'
Distinctive white flowers with broad, pale blue edging

C.c. 'Mrs V. Frère'
A dwarf plant. Flowers very flat, sculpted, rotate but with fine pointed tips, satiny, deep lavender, borne very freely. Lost but recently rediscovered in Sussex.

C.c. 'Queen of Sheba'
A big bold one. Open, loose growth to 45cm. Branched; flowers white with slight bluish tinge. Probably lost.

C.c. 'Queen of Somerville'
Free-flowering and producing, when mature, pale lavender-blue nearly flat, slightly cup-shaped flowers 6cm across, often with six divisions. 25cm in height.

C.c. 'Riverslea'
Introduced by Maurice Prichard. Height to 30cm. Flowers to 7cm across, deep purple-blue, up to eight pointed petals forming flat salver.

C.c. 'Samantha'
A new attractive miniature plant 10-15cm high with neat flowers 2cm across, pale blue with deeper blue rims to the petals.

C.c. 'Suzie'
Compact, low growing. Very pale blue flowers.

C.c. 'Thorpedo' (Torpedo) see C.c 'Blue Ball'

C.c. var. *turbinata*
In the wild this is covered with matted hairs, a characteristic transferred to some cultivars, which have subsequently been classified under this name.

C.c. var. *t.* 'Craven Bells'
Introduced by Reginald Farrer. An old selection has china-blue flowers of very round shape.

C.c. var. *t.* f. *alba* 'Hannah'
A tallish plant with many small bells.

C.c. var. *t.* 'Georg Arends'
Rich violet-blue flowers

C.c. var. *t.* 'Grandiflora'
As found in the wild has large, erect bell-shaped flowers 6cm across mid-violet and fading to almost white at the centres. Dull green leaves on a compact hummock.

C.c. var. *t.* 'Isabel'
Flat flowers in the form of a salver of one of the deepest blue colours to be found in the species or the genus.

C.c. var. *t.* 'Jewel'
Dark blue flowers. A vigorous plant to 30cm.

C.c. var. t. 'Karl Foerster'
Broad-spreading plant to 20cm high. Leaves 3cm long x 2.5cm, grass green. Flower stems 7-9cm, hairy. Flowers 4.5cm diameter, shallow cup-shaped, abundant, pale violet paling to even lighter violet, underside of petals veined and with deep purple trace. Long-flowering.

C.c. var. t. 'Pallida'
Very pale blue flowers, the plant covered with matted and curled hairs.

C.c. var. t. 'Wheatley Violet'
Neat plant to 20cm. Leaves dark green, hairy. Calyx and 6cm flower stems tinted burgundy. Large upturned cupped flowers 5cm across, violet.

C. cochleariifolia
This is strictly alpine, found in Pyrenees, Alps, and Balkan mountains but, as it grows anywhere - perhaps creeping too freely for some - it makes an easy garden plant anywhere with good drainage, such as the edge of paths. It has a long flowering period and is very suitable even for exposed containers. It is deciduous and very hardy. A creeping, branching rhizome throws up tufts of small round or heart-shaped leaves and stems with narrower leaves and topped by a single or one-sided cluster of 'Fairies' Thimbles'. These show wide variation in form and colour, though in the mountains this is a fairly constant mid-blue. Doubles occur spontaneously in gardens from time to time. Z6

C.c. var. alba
The white variety.

C.c. var. a. 'Bavaria White'
Pure white flowers on a compact plant. Selected for rapid growth from seed.

C.c. 'Bavaria Blue'
Flowers are dark blue, again on a compact plant, with rapid growth from seed.

C.c. 'Blue Tit'
From Blooms of Bressingham. China-blue.

C.c. 'Cambridge Blue'
From Blooms of Bressingham. This is the expected light blue.

C.c. 'Elizabeth Oliver'
A miniature double-flowered bun

C.c. 'Flore Pleno'
A double blue seedling that crops up from time to time unexpectedly; usually very pale blue.

C.c. 'Miss Willmott'
Named after the celebrated lady gardener of Warley in Essex, this has flowers of a mid greyish-blue with the faintest of silver fringes to the

mobcap.

C.c. 'Oakington Blue'
Introduced by Blooms of Bressingham. Deeper blue than 'Cambridge Blue' and with large flowers.

C.c. 'R. B. Loder'
Originated in the 1920s and was a slightly paler version of the double, 'Elizabeth Oliver'. The two are now confused.

C.c. 'Summer Pearl'
A compact, spreading plant, with a cushion 6cm high and flower stems to 10cm that bear, in spring, double palest blue-tinted white flowers, intermediate between 'Elizabeth Oliver' and 'Marion Fisher'.

C.c. 'Tubby'
Mid-blue; the bell is as wide as it is long, with the slightest reflexing of the petal tips.

C.c. 'White Baby'
Indistinguishable from *C.c.* var. *alba*.

C. 'Constellation'
Found as a seedling by Alan Bloom, this is probably a hybrid between *C. garganica* and *C. poscharskyana*. A truly hardy perennial, it has larger, more pointed and dentate leaves than the putative parents. It forms a large but un-invasive clump, 15cm x 60cm, throwing out each season a mass of 45cm leafy stems bearing many deep blue star-shaped flowers larger than those of either parent. It appears to set no seed but propagation is easy from pieces broken from the main cushion. It is excellent in hanging baskets. Z6

C. 'Covadonga'
Originally found and named by Clarence Elliott in the region of the Covadonga National Park in the north of Spain. The species has not been certainly determined but it is probably the shortest, neatest and deepest coloured of the harebell types and both extremely hardy and long-lived on a well-drained limestone rock garden. Height is 15-20cm. Z3

C. 'E. K. Toogood'
Probably a robust form or hybrid of *C. poscharskyana*, with its typical leaves and habit. The large rotate flowers are dark in hue, with a clear white centre. It is particularly suited to container or even hanging basket treatment, when its long stems are seen to advantage. 15 x 60cm. Z5

C. formanekiana AGM
From border mountains of Greece and Bulgaria, this is a biennial which is hardier that its origins might suggest, though in the garden it will grow where it is somewhat sheltered and with excellent drainage, such as a wall or well-

drained rockery. In such an environment it is frost-hardy. A stout taproot produces a silver-grey rosette of very neatly arrayed oval leaves, cordate and rounded at apex, and reminiscent of a decorative sempervivum. This rosette braves the winter to throw up a central stem and several decumbent branches bearing particularly large erect flowers in pale blue, pale pink or white. The whole plant is softly hairy and produces particularly beautiful flowers over a long period. In Scandinavia it is grown in pots as a houseplant, where the flowering period is especially long. 30 x 20 cm. Z7

C. garganica AGM
Italian mountains. This is a hardy alpine perennial that survives, frost-hardy, in a well-drained gritty soil. It is tufted, with small, evergreen, dentate heart-shaped leaves 1cm wide borne on short stems 10-15cm long and arranged in a tight bun. The abundant small flowers are rotate, about 1.5-2cm across, and mid-blue. Although seed is set most of the forms are kept true by taking cuttings. 12 x 15 cm. Z5

C.g. 'Blue Diamond'
This has a paler blue centre to the flower in the shape of a five-sided diamond.

C.g. subsp. *cephallenica*
Distinct in being especially hardy, larger in habit and flower size, with the latter a distinct pale grey-blue.

C.g. 'Dickson's Gold'
A well-known and popular miniature with golden leaves that both grow and show their gold best in full sun. It is slow to establish but robust.

C.g. 'Hirsuta'
The hairy leaves and stems give this form a grey appearance. Seedlings can revert. Propagation must be by cuttings.

C.g. 'W. H. Paine'
Has a striking white base to the flower.

C. 'Glandore' (syn *C. poscharskyana* 'Glandore')
Forms a tight cushion of deep violet-blue flowers.

C. glomerata
This species is native to a very wide area and varied habitats of Europe and Asia, with consequently different characteristics in cultivation. It is a sun-lover and has a strong preference for limey soils. In Britain it only occurs naturally on limestone. It tends to be short-lived, and is a copious seeder. It does not take easily to wet soils.

The leaves of the basal cluster are linear or lanceolate, somewhat similar to *C. persicifolia* but slightly more pointed. The stem can be from

10-60cm in height. It bears dense clusters, at the stem tip and in the axils of the stem-leaves, of mainly upward-pointing narrow bells with slightly flaring tips. Double forms have been described but as the flowers are already in clusters any additional effect is largely wasted. Z3

C.g. 'Compacta Alba'
A white-flowered form with particularly tight cushion.

C.g. var. *acaulis*
A very short-stemmed variant, very leafy, but with a good flower head.

C.g. var. *alba*
A white variety, also variable.

C.g. var. *a.* 'Alba Nana'
The name has been give to shorter selections of the above; there is no evidence of a fixed clone.

C.g. var *a.* 'Schneekrone' (Crown of Snow)
A distinct cultivar from Germany. It is some 50-60cm high, bearing copious clusters up its stem, all richly furnished with white flowers.

C.g. 'Caroline'
Has pale mauve pink flowers. Not a robust plant, it needs careful treatment and does not appear to be long-lived even with this. In recent years a not-dissimilar plant was found apparently wild on Salisbury Plain in Wiltshire.

C.g. var. *dahurica*
Came originally from S.E. Siberia; strong, tall stem with violet-blue flower heads copiously repeated in the stem leaf axils.

C.g. 'Joan Elliott'
Grows to 30-40cm and is a deep violet-blue. It sometimes needs some staking in exposed places.

C.g. 'Nana'
Dwarf. There are innumerable intermediates. Even totally isolated dwarfs give variable seedlings.

C.g. 'Purple Pixie'
Has bright violet-purple flowers with good stem clusters and is later flowering; it stands well. 40cm.

C.g. 'Superba' AGM
While any plant so labelled calls for suspicion, the original was a 60cm plant of striking violet blue, similar to *C.g.* var. *dahurica* in practice.

C.g. 'White Barn'
Introduced by Beth Chatto. The flower is not white but a strong blue, less violet than most.

Campanula glomerata

C. grossekii

From Hungary and named after Grossek, this unsurprisingly, from Reginald Farrer, picked up the reputation for being gross; it is very similar to *C. trachelium*. Distinguishing features are its bristly-branched stems, very hairy calyx, and bright yellow pollen. It comes from and favours similar conditions to the nettle-leaved bellflower: poor, stony or woodland soil. 90 x 30 cm. Z6

C. 'Hallii'

Originally a cross between *C. cochleariifolia* and *C. portenschlagiana* but evidence of the latter is hard to see; its appearance is of a taller, sparser and far-running white-flowered *C. cochleariifolia*. Height 10-12cm. Z5

C. x haylodgensis

Raised by Mr Anderson-Henry at Hay Lodge, Edinburgh in 1885, this was given as a hybrid between *C. carpatica* and *C. cochleariifolia*, and originally a single-flowered plant. Its subsequent history is undocumented, but the currently named *C. x haylodgensis* 'Plena' has double flowers of a pale blue. The flowers themselves differ from the not dissimilar 'Elizabeth Oliver' by being larger, more open and of deeper blue. The bright green leaves are also larger, and the plant has a more open habit. It is suggested that the *C. carpatica* influence here is the stronger. 15 x 10cm. Z5

C. x h. 'Marion Fisher'

A double white version and reported by the introducer as a seedling of 'Elizabeth Oliver'.

C. x h. 'Warley White'

A double white originally from Miss Willmott's garden near Brentwood in Essex over 100 years ago; is probably a hybrid.

C. x h. 'Yvonne'

Undistinguishable from the much older C. 'Tymonsii' to which it should be referred.

C. incurva

While this biennial comes from Greece and the Aegean islands it is hardy and can be grown in sheltered spots; best sown in pots and transferred to open ground. The basal rosette from a stout taproot gives branching stems that curve outward and upward and bear pale green heart-shaped to triangular leaves on longish but diminishing petioles. The large bulbous bells are pale blue or lilac, sometimes white, with reflexed borders to the petals. Sun, grit, limestone and perfect drainage are its friends, and it is frost-hardy to some -12°C if necessary. Z8

C. kemulariae

Caucasian endemic. This is allied to *C. raddeana* but has yellow pollen (the easiest means of distinguishing the two). It is perennial with a thick creeping rhizome, the basal cluster of leaves are a sharp-pointed oval with cordate base, doubly dentate and on petioles longer than the blade. Stems are 30cm long, much branched bearing smaller but similar leaves on shortening petioles. Flowers, open bells of a dullish blue, are on long pedicels. Best in poor, stony soil. 30 x 20+cm. Z4

C.k. alba
A white variant, slightly more compact.

C. 'Kent Belle'
Originating from Elizabeth Strangman, this is a recent hybrid, probably between *C. takesimana* and *C. latifolia*. Preferring a moist, shady situation, the creeping rootstock forms a mat, with dentate, heart-shaped leaves at base, diminishing as they ascend the stout 30cm stem. Bears clusters of glabrous, pendent tubular bells of a deep violet shade, rich and rare. Stems may be cut back for further flowering, and propagation is easy from the runners. 30 x 30cm. Z6

C. 'Kent Belle' variegated
A mutant shoot. Cream and purple splotched leaves, etc. Big blue flowers Jun-Sep. 1m. This is unstable and inclined to revert.

C. 'Kent Blue'
A seedling from 'Kent Belle', lighter in colour, retaining some gloss.

C. lactiflora
Comes from areas round the Black Sea. The large deep branching rootstock is fleshy but becomes gnarled and woody with age. A rosette of small, pale green basal leaves gives rise to a tall, stout stem up to 1.5m in height; this is clothed with oblong slightly dentate leaves and branches to produce a broad leafy panicle of erect flowers. These are each of modest size with flaring petals, commonly a pale, milky blue fading to white at the eye, that combine in the wide head to give the plant its distinctive character. In spite of its height, the plant needs staking only in wind-exposed sites. It is best seen *en masse*, as at Hidcote. The plant appreciates a deep, moist, humus-rich soil in full sun. Propagation is best from cuttings as they arise in spring; the rootstock may be divided brutally but only with some losses and the remains take two years or more to recover. Continuous flowering is assured if the main stems are cut back, allowing side stems to develop and repeat. 1.5m x 50cm. Z5

C.l. 'Alba' AGM
A white flowered form, correctly with dull or matt white flowers.

C.l. 'Blue Cross'
An average mid-blue.

C.l. 'Caerulea'
Has been named; china-blue.

C.l. 'Loddon Anna' AGM
A fine flesh-pink sport raised in Carlyle's Reading nursery in the 1920s.

C.l. 'Pouffe'
A dwarf type, not more than 30cm in height, with pale blue flowers.

C.l. 'Prichard's Variety' AGM
Raised by Maurice Prichard, this is the deepest blue of the species and has a slightly lighter centre. 75cm. Paler specimens are frequently sold under this name.

C.l. 'Superba' AGM
Extra large violet blue flowers; probably extinct.

C.l. 'White Pouffe'
A white-flowered, slightly more vigorous counterpart to 'Pouffe'

C. lanata
A handsome biennial, or monocarp, from the Balkans and northern Greece. It has large cordate pointed leaves that are grey-flannelled in appearance. The stem, to 65cm, is branched from the base, the branches often prostrate and incurved, the upper forming a pyramidal inflorescence of pale pink or cream flowers in the axils of the stem leaves. These flowers are also hairy inside and are of a good size, reminiscent of the Canterbury bell. Seed is set copiously and is the only method of propagation. The plant is frost-hardy but needs dry conditions to protect its woolliness from damp winters. 70 x 20cm. Z7

C. latifolia
A deciduous perennial, native to northern Britain and wide areas in Europe and Central Asia. It has a dense mass of fleshy roots forming a clump of oval to oblong leaves 10cm in length, which are pointed and coarsely dentate. These are on petioles of varying length that diminish in length on the leaves up the firm, straight, 1m high unbranched stems. Leaf and stem are slightly hairy, with few finer hairs rather than the coarse hairs of the somewhat similar *C. trachelium*. Borne in the leaf-axils, and also in a terminal cluster, are the tubular bell-shaped flowers up to 7cm in length. These are pendent or upright and either light blue or pale lavender in colour. In Switzerland it is said to be a marker of slightly acid soils, growing in woodland and lush meadows, often in partial shade, but in cultivation it

is not at all demanding. Propagation is by division in the spring, or from the abundant seed. 90 x 30cm. Z3

C.l. var. ***alba***
Has white flowers, ideally without blue shading at the base.

Campanula latifolia

C.l. 'Brantwood'
From John Ruskin's garden on the shores of Lake Coniston in the English Lake District, this bears well formed horizontally held flowers in a deep violet blue.

C.l. 'Gloaming'
Originally from Alan Bloom, this is a pleasing pure, light smoky blue. 80cm.

C.l. var. *macrantha*
Large, deep blue flowers. The stem is tall, with long internodes, making for a somewhat bare, gaunt plant.

C.l. var. *macrantha alba*
A white counterpart, also rather clumsy.

C.l. 'Pallida'
Pale blue, somewhat unstable.

C.l. 'Roger Wood'
From Thelma Kaye, a well-known Hardy Planter in Cheshire; bears bi-coloured violet and white flowers.

C.l. 'White Ladies' (*C.l.* var. *alba* 'White Ladies')
From Alan Bloom. A tall plant with long (to 10cm) flowers, flared at petal tips, of the purest white, including the eye, and has a longer flowering period than most.

C. latiloba
Related to *C. persicifolia*, and is sometimes classified as a sub-species. It looks coarser and more robust. The mostly evergreen basal rosettes are similar but larger and formed in clumps of long narrow lanceolate leaves with slightly winged petioles. The most obvious distinction is that the flowers are held on very short pedicels and close to the stiff, thick, angular stem, which can be up to 10cm in diameter. The flowers are widely bell-shaped, to 5cm across, and deep blue. Flowering is over a long period, and this is a good subject for cutting back and repeat flowering. 80 x 30cm. Z3

C.l. 'Alba' AGM
The white form.

C.l. 'Highcliffe Variety' AGM
Selected by Prichard. A strong grower with rich lavender violet flowers.

C.l. 'Percy Piper' AGM
From Blooms, is slightly more dwarf, but hard to distinguish from 'Highcliffe Variety'. It was said to be a hybrid with *C. persicifolia*.

Campanula latiloba

C. medium (Canterbury bell)

This is a biennial, native to the border of France and Italy but which has become widely naturalised, even in Britain - especially along railway tracks. In the first year plants form a rosette of roughly hairy, notched and stalkless leaves followed, in the second season, by an erect stem from the stout taproot. This stem is much branched, in height up to 90cm, and bears large, showy 6cm flowers which are wide at the base, almost square in section, the stubby, flaring petals recurved at their rims. Colour in the wild is white or lilac but breeding has brought in a wide range of shades. Propagation is uniquely from seed, which should be sown in early summer in pots or the open, potted up later, and given some winter protection; kept under cover they provide early colour but may be planted out as bedding, preferably *en masse*, in the border. Colours are nearly rainbow-wide: dark rose, pink, lilac, lavender, pale and dark blue, and white.

There are doubles of two sorts: hose-in-hose (two rows of petals), and cup-and-saucer (*C.m.* 'Calycanthema' AGM, where the calyx has become petaloid). The seed strains evolved bear many names, with colour variation as wide as the singles. The flamboyant effect is not the fashion it was in the past, partly because the flowering period is not as long as with some bedding plants, though deadheading is rewarding if tedious. 80 x 30cm. Z8

C. 'Mist Maiden'

Of obscure origins but is similar to *C. rotundifolia*, with a delicacy that makes it distinct; it has been suggested that it is a hybrid with *C. tommasiniana*. It is a vigorous, hardy perennial, a herbaceous clump that spreads slowly but does not appear to seed. It resembles in every way a refined harebell, with slender pale green 30cm stems and finely figured white pendent flowers with flared mouths. It spreads slowly by underground runners, and these are used for propagation in spring as growth restarts. Z5

C. 'Mystery'

This is an unidentified plant that needs taxonomic investigation. Though catalogued under Campanula in the trade, it bears a number of characteristics atypical to the point of exclusion – foliage distinct from any known species, petals not united at base, petals unlike any species, anthers semi-fused, unusual growth habit, etc, etc. The bootlace petals are pale pink. Spreads when content, but dislikes winter damp. 80cm. Z8

C. 'Mystery in Blue'

This is in all points like the preceding, but with blue petals. 80cm. Z8

This and 'Mystery', along with *C. takesimana* 'Beautiful Trust', are similar in most points and no doubt related. Taxonomic investigation and identification is needed. From USA.

C. ochroleuca

Sometimes considered a sub-species of *C. alliariifolia*, this is quite distinct in the garden, where it makes perennial groundcover of an unusual shade of pale green heart-shaped leaves bearing creamy yellow flowers. Standing some 30cm high, it forms a dense, floppy cushion on a well-drained, rocky slope. Z6

C.o. **'White Bells'** A white-flowered selection.

C. patula

Grows widely in northern and central Europe and is one of the few British natives, now very rare and found only in some shaded western valleys. It is a biennial with a fine, fibrous root system, with thin, dry stems and leaves. The latter are oblong, wider at the tips, notched at the edges, the blade narrowing to a short stalk. Stem leaves are stalkless, their stems branching and spreading and bearing numerous star-shaped flowers, in their best forms of a luminous rose-purple, and also paler and even a rare white. Height is to 30cm or more. Propagation is from seed, which is not easy to obtain. Z6

C. persicifolia

Widespread over Europe, The plant seen in the wild is a poor thing compared with the cultivars we know so well. Growing in alpine meadows it could be mistaken for a stunted *C. carpatica*, both in height and flower appearance, and in this highly competitive environment prolific seeding, a feature of the genus, is essential to survival in an environment where grasses and other competition could quickly stifle its growth. It is also reliably hardy.

This is probably the most widely grown of the entire genus, largely because of the cultivars, which have been so popular. Names are legion, and many of those found in old - and not so old - literature are either unknown or uncertain because of the inadequate descriptions in these catalogues - descriptions of either impossible or irresponsible interpretation.

In cultivation there is, as with others, the fact to be kept in mind that hardly ever does it sow true, and even in cultivation where a flower is self-pollinated by hand, few if any of the resultant seedlings will resemble the parent. Unless there are facilities for micro-propagation it is only by division or cuttings that a particular clone can be preserved. This, as a rule is, of course, no different from any other genus but the tendency to short life of a campanula makes it the more significant. Success depends upon good cultivation, adequate feeding, and frequent moving and division.

The height of all plants will depend on position and soil conditions, among other variables, and, varying considerably, should not be used diagnostically. Moreover, many of the plants found in lists and publications will be synonyms of others, and, being without adequate diagnostic descriptions, will not be valid. Current naming is an even more dangerous minefield than that of *C. carpatica* cultivars. Z3

C.p. alba
This name simply denotes a white-flowered plant.

C.p. 'Alba Coronata' (syn *C.p.* 'Alba Plena')
Again, this name covers any double white flowered plant.

C.p. 'Bennett's Blue'
From Richard Blenkinship (formerly of Orchard Nurseries, Grantham, Lincolnshire). A vigorous plant of 80-100cm stems with pale blue double flowers of two to three rows of petals.

C.p. 'Blue Bloomers'
Has two rows of loose, blowsy petals of dark blue-violet.

C.p. 'Boule de Neige'
Never vigorous and a martyr to rust, this is now probably extinct. The flowers have four or more sets of rounded, incurved petals, which give the appearance of a double rose with, of course, no perfume! 'Fleur de Neige' is frequently confused with this.

C.p. 'Chettle Charm' (syn *C.p.* 'George Chiswell')
Distributed by Blooms has 60-75cm stems bearing white flowers with blue edging. It appears to be vigorous.

C.p. 'Coronata'
A semi-double cup-in-cup, the bell somewhat square in section.

C.p. 'Fleur de Neige' AGM
Bears large tightly packed flowers with three rows of petals and petaloid stamens that are pointed at the tips. Rust resistant.

C.p. 'Flore Pleno'
Has double blue flowers.

C.p. 'Frances'
Has about three rows of fringed white petals tinged with the slightest blue.

C.p. 'Frank Lawley'
A medium-sized rich blue flower with two sets of petals, the outer of which is acutely reflexed, giving a shuttlecock effect.

C.p. 'Gawen'
A short but vigorous plant with white cup-and-saucer flowers similar to 'Hampstead White', though smaller.

C.p. 'Grandiflora' (var. *grandiflora* but without botanical authority) Large-flowered.

C.p. 'Grandiflora Alba' (var. *grandiflora alba*, but without botanical authority) Large white flowers.

C.p. 'Hampstead White' (syn = 'Hetty')
A relatively old cultivar, 80cm. It has flowers with two rows of petals in cup-and-saucer form, their veins and tips tinged with green.

C.p. Irish double white
Full double white flowers with a green button centre Jun-Aug and later, 45cm. Not a strong grower. Found by Stephen Taffler.

C.p. 'Kelly's Gold'
Golden foliage; white single flowers touched with blue at edge of petals.

C.p. 'La Belle'
Has double, bell-shaped blue flowers.

C.p. 'Moerheimii'
From Holland, has very double white flowers on stout 75cm stems. It is very close to the true 'Fleur de Neige'

C.p. var. *planiflora*
A miniature, a genetic recessive, with stout stem for its size, dark green congested leaves, and large, rather clumsy looking flowers

C.p. var. *planiflora* f. *alba*
Similar to the last, with white flowers. It appears to be commoner than the blue. Both give abundant seed, a large percentage of which reverts to give normal sized plants.

C.p. 'Pride of Exmouth'
An old cultivar of uncertain origin. Strong straight stems to 80-100cm bear deep blue double flowers with three to four sets of petals. Similar in form to 'Bennett's Blue' but deeper in colour.

C.p. 'Rearsby Belle'
Introduced after ten years' breeding by Hazel Kaye of Kaye's Garden Nursery, Rearsby; it has tall, upright stems and is a blue equivalent of the cup-and-saucer 'Hampstead White'.

C.p. 'Telham Beauty'
Almost certainly extinct, since the original is recorded as perishing without propagation, this was a very vigorous plant with an abundance of singularly

large flowers. Well documented at the time, it proved to be genetically a
tetraploid. Both it and a white variant were lost.

C.p. 'Tinkerbell'
From Hazel Kaye of Kaye's Garden Nursery, is a cup-and-saucer with
small delicate white flowers. 60cm.

C.p. variegated Leaves speckled and rimmed cream. From USA.

C.p. white cup and saucer
An all-embracing variable description.

C.p. 'Wirral Belle'
A deep blue double.

C.p. 'Wortham Belle'
Traceably the same as the earlier 'Bennett's Blue', the prior name.

There are many other cultivars offered, named incidentally,
masquerading under a new name, inadequately described, and duplicates
of existing cultivars.

C. portenschlagiana AGM
Comes from the Balkan mountains and in the garden can be a modest
menace due to its underground creeping habit but is not hard to control. A
small but fleshy rootstock puts up one or many 5cm across rosettes of tiny
heart-shaped leaves on long petioles; these leaves are often multiply-serrate
and wavy at full size, the tip rounded. Stems up to 40cm long bearing
similar but stalkless leaves are thrown out from the stock, with side stems in
their axils bearing the numerous flowers. These are funnel-shaped bells
cleft to half way, with the lobes flexed outward at about 45°. The flowers
are of a uniform deep lavender. The plant is ideal in a wall or paving but in
any case needs a stony site in sun. Z4

C.p. 'Major'
Has larger flowers.

C.p. 'Resholdt's Variety'
Is larger in all its parts, and a brighter, almost luminous, colour.

C. poscharskyana
Also from the Balkan mountains and, although it resembles the above in
many respects, the most obvious difference is the flower shape, which here
is rotate. The leaves are smaller and on shorter petioles; the leaf dentation is
finer and they tend to be more hairy. The flowering stems are also longer.
Flowers are cleft to three-quarters or more of their length, which gives them
an open star-shape. This plant has a long flowering period, especially when
the long stems are shorn back as flowers fade and wither; it behaves well in

containers and is effective tumbling over edges. It has also an attractive scandent habit when grown against a sunny wall or bank. 25 x 30cm. Z3

C.p. 'Albiflora'
Has white flowers; often confused with 'E H Frost'.

C.p. 'Blauranke'
A German selection; deep violet with a clear white eye to the flower.

C.p. 'E. H. Frost' (syn *C.p.* 'Elizabeth Holister Frost')
Milky-white flowers.

C.p. 'Glandore' see C. 'Glandore'

C.p. 'Lilacina'
Has lilac flowers.

C.p. 'Lisduggan'
Found in a southern county of Ireland, has mauve-pink flowers. It is as hardy but somewhat less vigorous than the type.

C.p. 'Multiplicity'
Has double blue flowers.

C.p. 'Schneeranke'
Has snow-white flowers, whiter than 'E H Frost'.

C.p. 'Stella' AGM
Large flowers of a deep violet on 40cm stems. It is said that this is a hybrid with *C. garganica* from Georg Arends.

C. primulifolia
A short-lived perennial from the Western Mediterranean region - Portugal, in the Algarve and Beira areas, and also the adjacent areas of Spain. The basal rosette resembles very closely that of the common primrose. Pale flowers with a white eye. 85 x 25cm. Z8

C. 'Puff of Smoke'
From Bob Brown of Cotswold Garden Flowers, this is *C. punctata* x *C. latifolia* 'Macrantha'. Large, smoky-blue buds open to white flowers. 60cm. Z7

C. punctata
Originates in Japan and, to a lesser extent, in Siberia and eastern China. It is very hardy. It is also very variable, but is characterised by the flowers, tubular bells speckled or spotted on the inside and, in many cases, the outside but in very varying degrees. The creeping rootstock throws up rosettes of fleshy, pointed heart-shaped leaves on long petioles in spring, and stiff stems up to 40cm bearing similar but stalkless leaves and tubular bell-shaped flowers about 5cm long, the tips of whose petals are not usually reflexed; the bright green calyx, which lies flat to the corolla, is therefore

prominent, especially as the flowers are pendent. Best in sun or part shade. To 50 x 30cm.

This species is difficult to distinguish from *C. takesimana,* and, as they are cross-fertile, they have largely lost their distinctiveness in the garden. No doubt some botanist will unite them sometime.

C.p. f. *albiflora*
The flowers are pure white.

C.p. f. *a.* 'Nana Alba'
A dwarf with white flowers.

C.p. 'Alina's Double'
Rich pink hose-in-hose flowers, having darker spots within.

C.p. 'Cherry Bells'
From the USA. Has a strong upright habit and plenty of red colour. It is a selected f. *rubriflora.* (This is difficult to distinguish from *C. takesimana* 'Elizabeth', if indeed at all different.)

C.p. var. *chinensis*
From China and Siberia. Has shorter and finer stems, and smaller flowers with less rich markings.

C.p. hose-in-hose
Some 60cm tall, with doubled pale to reddish bells. It is a strong grower like all of its species, and is treated similarly in all points.

C.p. var. *hondoensis*
The Japanese variety. It is in general considerably larger in all its parts than the typical Siberian variety.

C.p. 'Hot Lips'
From the USA, this has the burgundy markings densest toward the lips of the corolla.

C.p. f. *impunctata*
A dwarf plant. The flowers are almost pure white apart from one small spot on the tip of each petal. It has been distributed as f. *alba* 'Nana Alba'.

C.p. var. *microdonta*
Is smaller, paler and the whole plant more glabrous.

C.p. 'Millenium'
Large brown-pink marked creamy-white bells, 30cm.

C.p. 'Milly'
A very attractive miniature about 15cm high, less rampant than others, and suitable for any situation where its diminutive size will not be swamped by taller plants, but is best in a container.

C.p. 'Nana'
A dwarf 15cm plant.

C.p. 'Pantaloons'
Hose-in-hose pale purple flowers on upright stems to 80cm.

C.p. 'Pink Chimes'
A compact form with 5cm bells speckled dark purple, especially at the mouth.

C.p. f. *rubriflora*
Veining on the outside of the corolla is also red, while the internal colouring is deeper and more liberally scattered, giving a much darker red impression overall.

C.p. 'Wedding Bells'
A 50cm high plant with hose-in-hose flowers of creamy pink with darker spots.

C.p. white hose-in-hose
Some 30cm tall. Bells of a creamy white with very faint pink spots inside the flowers.

C.p. 'Wine 'n Rubies'
Large flowers heavily speckled dark red-purple.

C. pyramidalis
The Chimney Bellflower, from Northeast Italy and the adjacent Balkan area. This perennial, very short-lived and, treated as biennial, is easy from seed. The basal rosette is of broadly ovate dentate leaves on long petioles. The stem, to 1.2m in the wild and potentially more in cultivation, bears oval to lanceolate, stalkless leaves, and a pyramid of numerous flowering spikes. The long pedicels hold the small flowers erect; the style protrudes from the flower, which is deep lobed and rotate. The whole plant is glabrous. In the garden it self-sows modestly, always choosing crevices or gravel in which to grow; usually inconvenient spots from which it is hard, if not impossible, to transfer it. There are blue and white variants. Z8

C.p. 'Aureovariegata'
A variant with yellow blotched leaves; it is not stable, and the variegation may be due to a virus.

C. raddeana.
Caucasus. From running roots arise mats of rosettes of shiny cordate leaves on long petioles, followed by fine stems with a wine-coloured tinge; these bear similar leaves on shorter petioles and terminate in short racemes of pendent dark blue deep-lobed bells. The pollen is characteristically orange. Being a runner in stony soils, it is easily propagated in spring from runners with a rosette attached. 30 x 20cm. Z6

Campanula pyramidalis

C. rapunculoides

"The most insatiable and irrepressible of beautiful weeds" opined Reginald Farrer: a just assessment. It proliferates by rampant roots and abundant seeding and, when happy, renders the gardener most unhappy. The mass of white roots spreads widely, deeply and rapidly; the stems rise about 90 cm from a basal rosette of heart-shaped pointed leaves on long stalks; the stem-leaves are stalkless and broadly lance-shaped. The stems are set with pendent blue flowers 2cm long with slightly flaring petals. These are often prone to be held toward one side of the stem. 90 x 30+cm. Z3

Cultivation of this beautiful weed should be in a confined area and stems cut down before seed has set. Gardeners on light soils need to take greater precautions than those with clay.

One of the worst aspects of this plant is that it is frequently offered under other names, both under *Campanula* and, especially, *Adenophora*. It is worthwhile taking a flower (if necessarily surreptitiously) and peeling away the petals; *Adenophora* will have a small disc at the base of and surrounding the style; *Campanula* will not. *Caveat emptor!*

C.r. 'Afterglow'

This has pink flowers but is even more rare than the white. It is only 15-20cm in height, and, unfortunately, has not the vigour of the blue. Seed, if set, is not viable

C.r. 'Alba'

A rare white selection, a little shorter than the blue; it does not creep like the type, nor does it seem to set viable seed

C. rapunculus

Possibly native to the south of England. Formerly its root was used as a vegetable, as it still is in some parts of Europe. The most useful vegetable clones appear to have been largely lost to cultivation but it is an attractive if unspectacular biennial when grown, seeding itself when happy. The 60cm flowering stem from an insignificant rosette of oval leaves bears many small pale blue pendent bells. This is the rampion of the brothers Grimm story of Rapunzel, and the plant from which *C. rapunculoides* - 'rapunculus-like', gets a name - but not its modesty. The root is said to be good eating, either raw or cooked, and to have a pungent, nutty flavour. 75 x 25 cm. Z6

C. rhomboidalis

Botanically closely related to the harebell, a perennial with fleshy roots, diamond shaped basal leaves, a stem some 45cm high bearing similar leaves without petioles, and a raceme of rich purple-blue bell-shaped 2-3cm long flowers. It is best grown in bold sweeps but spreads very slowly. Propagation may be from seed or by division of the rootstock. *C.r.* Gorter has been recorded as being synonymous with *C. rapunculoides* but *C.r.* Linnaeus is treated quite separately in Floras of Asia and is quite distinct. Z5

Campanula rotundifolia

C. rotundifolia

The harebell: the type plant not only for the genus but also the family *Campanulaceae*. It is circumpolar in origin and found down to Mediterranean latitudes. Being so widespread, it has collected multiple regional names, all variations on a theme and, of course, all cross-fertile. More than thirty have been described but, unless collected with careful botanical observation in a known area and kept isolated in cultivation, they are all interfertile and lose their distinguishing characteristics in the garden.

The round basal leaves of the specific name are variable from truly round to heart-shaped, and wither at flowering time. The stem is fine and 15-30cm in height. Stem leaves are needle-shaped and without petioles. Flowers are variable in shade around mid-blue, usually fine, pendent narrow bells and one to several per stem. In the wild it is found in rough, stony impoverished soils, acid or basic, and will do best in the garden in similar impeccably drained positions. It is likely to seed copiously. Dwarf forms have been found but most tend to lose this characteristic in cultivation, which is usually in too rich a soil. Z3

C.r. var. *alba*
A white variant that comes mostly true from seed.

C.r. 'Flore Pleno'
Has two rows of frilly-edged petals; it is not robust.

C.r. 'Mingan'
Hails from Canada, a natural dwarf sport collected in the Arctic and one that keeps its miniature habit in cultivation. Others that are similar, but which usually fail to keep their dwarf proportions in cultivation, include vars. *alaskana* and *groenlandica*.

C.r. 'Olympica'
From the Washington Olympics in the USA. Particularly robust. 25cm tall, with darkish green, dentate leaves

Other close relatives sometimes offered include *C. baumgartenii*, *C. carnica*, *C. justiniana*, *C. recta* and *C.scheuchzeri*.

C. 'Sarastro'
A new hybrid between *C. punctata* and *C. trachelium* introduced by Staudengaertnerei Sarastro in Germany, Large hairy leaves and large pendulous deep smoky-blue bells. A clumper. Height 60cm. A compact improvement on *C.* 'Kent Belle'.

C. sarmatica
Caucasus. From the single rootstock, a large clump of coarse, wrinkled and crumpled, hairy grey-green leaves, triangular and pointed in shape with cordate base and petioles longer than leaf-blades, gives rise to several stout unbranched hairy stems bearing similar but smaller and stemless leaves. The hairy bell-shaped grey-blue flowers with reflexed lobes are held horizontally. Height is 30-40cm. The plant is unattractive to slugs, as are most of the hairier species. Division is impossible, cuttings difficult, so propagation is by seed. Z5

C. 'Smokey Blue'

From Bob Brown of Cotswold Garden Flowers. Like an upright bushy *C. punctata*, with smoky-blue pendent flowers. 55cm. Z6

C. speciosa

Eastern Pyrenees and southern Massif Central of France. This can be monocarpic or short-lived perennial. A large flat rosette of lanceolate leaves throws up a stout stem with narrow bristly stalkless leaves. The large bell-shaped blue flowers, reminiscent of the Canterbury Bell, are borne on pedicels that are long below but decrease in length up the stem, giving the effect of a pyramidal spike. Best raised from seed and in pots for planting out in spring. In a warm but poorer, preferably gritty and basic soil, this is a rewarding plant. 45 x 30cm. Z8

C. takesimana

This was first introduced to cultivation from a collection in the Korean island of Ullung Do in the Sea of Japan. It is related to *C. punctata*, to which it is quite similar. It is likely that they are so closely related that the two have crossed in the garden, and distinguishing between them is now far from easy. They share a strongly creeping rootstock which throws up at intervals rosettes of fleshy stems with bright glossy green leaves with markedly veined surfaces; both stems and leaves often have a reddish tinge. The flowering stems are between 45 and 60cm in height, and bear handsome pendent tubular bells of greyish-pink with maroon inner markings. The shades vary but are usually deeper within the bell, as with *C. punctata*. One of the best forms has been named 'Elizabeth', but there are paler forms that have been called 'Pallida' etc. with little authority. The plant is deciduous and hardy, but can be very rampant in lighter soils. While appreciating moisture it does not like excessive damp and preference is for neutral soils. All forms are most easily propagated from the runners; seed is set, but it rarely spreads by this means. Z7

C.t. 'Beautiful Trust'

Found in Korea and named by the discoverer 'Beautiful Truth' after his daughter, this name having been subsequently misread. It is a curiosity with fine light coloured spidery petals, usually more numerous than the customary five of *Campanula* and by its form recalling *Michauxia*. It is as vigorous as the type, though the stems, with abundant flowers, are a little shorter.

C.t. 'Elizabeth'

This is one of the best selections of *C. takesimana*; it was first distributed from the nursery of Elizabeth Strangman in Kent. It is a strong plant, growing up to 60cm or more, bearing bells of deep red with deeper maroon markings both within and outside of the bells, which can be up to 9cm in length.

C. thyrsoides

One of the pale yellow bellflowers, though of a greenish persuasion. The basal rosette of wavy, lance-shaped leaves gives rise to stout erect stem with shortening, closely-packed bristly leaves, again lance-shaped, terminating as bracts beneath the inflorescence arranged in a steeple-like thyrse of tight-packed pale flowers. The flower colour is pale straw, but there is a regional subspecies, subsp. *carniolica*, from the eastern Alps, which is more yellow. 90 x 30 cm. Z5.

C. trachelium (syn = C. urticifolia)

Has various common names: nettle-leaved bellflower, Coventry bells, bats-in-the-belfry. It is native to much of Europe and Asia, including Britain, where it grows though not now abundantly, roughly south of a line from Wash to Severn. It has a woody rootstock from which emerge one or a few stems that are rough and acutely angled and grow to 1m or more. The leaves are nettle-shaped and bristly, happily without the sting; the lower are on long, the upper on shorter petioles, the leaves diminishing in size upward. Flowers are tubular, bell-shaped and more or less hairy, with corolla lobes divided to about one-third. In comparison, the flowers are rather similar to those of *C. latifolia*, but rather more hairy and shorter. The impression is of a slightly weedy, coarse plant that looks best when naturalised in grass or woodland, where it is less invasive at the root though it seeds freely. Propagation is easiest from seed, which can result in white or blue flowered plants. Cultivars can be increased by cuttings of the new shoots in spring. 80 x 30 cm. Z3

C.t. var. alba

The white-flowered variety.

C.t. 'Alba Flore Pleno'

A white double-flowered form and a delicious cottage garden plant. It is as tall and strong as the type, and sets seed although few, if any, of the resulting seedlings will bear double white flowers - indeed a lot of them will not even be white. Division is the only way to propagate; courage is needed to slice through the woody rootstock with a sharp knife but if done in spring as new growth is commencing or in early autumn by carefully teasing the roots apart, most divisions will produce healthy plants the following season. New plants will be even more numerous and vigorous if the stems are cut back before flowering, when at the cost of one season's flowers a greater number of divisions will be produced.

Campanula trachelium 'alba Flore Pleno'

C.t. 'Bernice'
Known since the late 16th century but introduced into Britain from Holland much more recently, this is a cultivar with deep amethyst-blue multiple flowers with up to four sets of petals. It flowers profusely for a long time with the flowers held well above the leaves and is both tough and hardy.

Like its white counterpart it can be propagated by division. Only a very tiny percentage might come true from seed.

C.t. 'Snowball'
A name applied in USA; 'Alba Plena' is correct, especially as 'Snowball' is illegitimate, a confusing translation of a *C. persicifolia* cultivar of old date.

C. 'Tymonsii'
This is said to be a hybrid between *C. carpatica* and *C. pyramidalis* though it retains little obvious evidence of either; it is none the less valuable and worthy, particularly as it is probably the latest of all campanulas to flower in a season, in addition to being one of the truest blues of the genus. A slowly spreading mat of toothed oval bluntly pointed leaves on glossy green stems some 10cm high are thickly topped by open, shallow bells of china-blue. The plant is ideal for sinks and troughs and is both hardy and long-lived. Propagation is from the runners. Z4

C. 'Van-Houttei'
Named for van Houtte, one-time curator of Ghent botanic garden, this is an old hybrid between *C. latifolia* and *C. punctata*, the reverse cross from *C.* 'Burghaltii'. In 'Van-Houttei' the *latifolia* is the seed parent. Similar in habit to 'Burghaltii', with 10cm long, notched and hairy leaves and flower buds a deep inky colour opening to indigo blue similar to that of the now better-known 'Kent Belle'. 45 x 25cm. Z4

C. versicolor
A mountain plant from western Greece, Albania, Balkans and southeast Italy. From a fleshy root, which becomes large and woody, the basal leaves, on long petioles, are leathery, olive green, oval-heart-shaped and notched. Upper leaves are smaller and narrower and the petioles shorter. The leafy 30-50cm stems end in spikes of open flowers that are clearly bi-coloured, of a pale blue or white but with deep violet-blue centres and edgings. It is variable in its colouring, some clones being much more distinctive than others.

The plant is obviously a close relative of the much taller *C. pyramidalis* and has been described by some as a subspecies of it. It usually sets abundant seed. 40 x 20cm Z8

C. vidalii (Properly *Azorina vidalii*, and separated by Feer in 1890 as being the only shrubby member of the genus.)
A perennial from the Azores with the distinction of never being blue but white or, more commonly, pale or deep pink. A single woody stem with several side stems from low down, all scarred with the hardened bases of dead leaves, give rise to rosettes of glossy notched linear leaves with indented veins. These elongate to form flowering spikes of nodding and

characteristically waisted recurved bells some 3cm in length. These are white or pink, sometimes a variegation of the two. At the base of the flower is the bright orange disc of the top of the ovary. This is not strictly a garden plant as it is not frost-hardy but it will be the better for being outside for a great part of the year. 45 x 40cm. Z9

C. 'Warley White' (incorrectly 'Warleyensis')

Mentioned under *C. carpatica* but is probably a hybrid between it and *C. cochleariifolia*. It was claimed to be a white seedling of *C.* x *haylodgensis*. It is a lax plant with 20cm stems that tumble prostrately around the basal tuft of heart-shaped leaves. The stems bear similar, sparse leaves; all are of a characteristic yellowish-green shade, which in *Campanula* is usually a sign of a hybrid plant. The flowers are semi- or fully-double, about 4cm across, and open almost flat to the sun. The plant is best grown in semi-shade or where winter sun will not stimulate it into precocious growth, with subsequent weakening of the plant when exposed to alternating freezing and wet conditions. Such repetition rapidly exhausts this and many other small campanulas, giving them a reputation of tenderness. Z5

C. x *wockei* 'Puck'

Introduced by Alan Bloom of Bressingham, this is said to be a natural hybrid, probably between *C. pulla* and *C. waldsteiniana* but accounts of its origin are obscure.

It is a very hardy deciduous perennial from alpine areas of the Northern Balkans. A winter-resting bud from underground runners gives rise to tiny wedge-shaped leaves and a rosette of ovate leaves with a stem 10cm high bearing lanceolate leaves. The flower is a single dark-blue pendent bell. It is modestly mat-forming, and is propagated by this means. Z5

C. 'Yvonne'

This is undistinguishable from the much older *C.* x *tymonsii*, to which it should be referred.

Hardiness Zones

These are quoted for those who find them useful. European gardeners will be more concerned with local microclimate for their plants: situations affected by exposure to sun or wind; drainage, air and soil moisture, frost exposure etc.

Zone	Average Minimum Winter Temperature
3	-40 to -34°C
4	-34 to -29°C
5	-29 to -23°C
6	-23 to -18°C
7	-18 to -12° C
8	-12 to -7°C
9	-7 to -1° C
10	-1 to 4°C
11	above 4° C

Further Reading

For the species:-
Bailey, L. H. *A Garden of Bellflowers* New York, 1953
Blamey, M. & Grey-Wilson, C. *The Illustrated Flora of Britain & Northern Europe* London, 1989
----- *Mediterranean Wild Flowers* London, 1993
Bowles, E. A. *My Garden in Summer* London, 1914, 1998
Crook, Clifford H. *Campanulas, their Cultivation and Classification* Country Life, 1951
----- *Campanulas & Bellflowers in Cultivation* London, 1959
Correvon, H. *The Genus Campanula* The Garden, 1901
Farrer, R. *The English Rock Garden* 1918
Griffiths, M. *Index of Garden Plants* London, 1964
Prichard, M. *The Genus Campanula* RHS Journal, 1902
Many further references will be found in the various European, Mediterranean, Turkish and Russian Floras.

For species and cultivars:-
Brickell, C. (ed.) *RHS A-Z Encyclopaedia of Garden Plants* London, 1996

For cultivars:-
Bloom, A. *Hardy Perennials* London, 1957
----- *Perennials for Trouble-Free Gardening* London, 1960
----- *Hardy Perennials* London, 1991
Huxley, A. (ed.). *The New RHS Dictionary of Gardening*.
Lewis, P. E. &. Lynch, M. *Campanulas* London, 1989; revised 1998.

For pests & diseases: -
Buczacki, S & Harris, K. *Collins Guide to Pests, Diseases and Disorders of Garden Plants* London, 1985

Web Sites:-
The RHS Plant Finder* www.rhs.org.uk/rhsplantfinder
The Hardy Plant Society www.hardy-plant.org.uk.
Many nurseries have their own web sites; for addresses of these see *The RHS Plant Finder*
*It should be borne in mind that names given in *The RHS Plant Finder* have been sifted botanically, but all entries are based, unchecked, on information supplied by the nurserymen offering the plants.

Where to see and buy Campanulas

Campanulas may be seen in many gardens. Two NCCPG National Collections® offer wide selections, including plant sales: -
Burton Agnes Hall, Nr Driffield, E. Yorkshire (see below) has a 'Campanula Garden' within the larger Elizabethan Garden with great variety on show in season.
Lingen Nursery, Lingen, Nr. Bucknell, Shropshire. (see below).
A number may still be seen at Padlock Croft, West Wratting, Nr Cambridge.
The great gardens, such as Hidcote and Kiftsgate in Gloucestershire have good displays

SEED is available from a few general suppliers but beware packets offered as named cultivars:-
Chiltern Seeds, Bortree Stile, Ulverston, Cumbria LA12 7PB
Thompson & Morgan Ltd, Poplar Lane, Ipswich, Suffolk IP8 3BU (www.thompson-morgan.com)
Plant World, St. Marychurch Road, Newton Abbott, S. Devon TQ124SE
B & T World Seeds, Internet catalogue; mail order:- www.b-and-t-world-seeds.com

The main sources will always be the Specialist Societies (lists available to members only) especially:-
Alpine Garden Society, Sec. AGS Centre, Avon Bank, Pershore, Worcestershire WR10 3JP
Cottage Garden Society, Membership Sec., 244 Eddleston Road, Crewe, Cheshire CW2 7EJ
Hardy Plant Society, Administrator, Little Orchard, Great Comberton, Pershore, Worcestershire WR10 3DP

PLANTS may often be found for sale at many of the gardens that open for visitors, including those of the NCCPG National Collections ®:-
Burton Agnes Hall, Burton Agnes, Driffield, E. Yorkshire YO25 0ND
Lingen Nursery and Garden, see below.

The following selected nurseries in the UK offer catalogues, and (*) mail order.
Avondale Nursery, Earlsdon, Coventry, Warwickshire CV5 6DZ,
☏ 024 766 73662 *

Beeches Nursery, Village Centre, Ashdon, Saffron Walden, Essex CB10 2HB ☎ 01799 584 362 *

Bressingham Garden Centre, Bressingham, Diss, Norfolk IP22 2AB 01379 688480 (and at Borde Hill, Windsor and Peterborough)

Charter House Nursery, 2 Nunwood, Dumfries, DG2 0HX ☎ 01387 720 363 *

Cotswold Garden Flowers, Sands Lane, Badsey, Evesham, Worcestershire WR11 5EZ ☎ 01386 422829*

Elworthy Cottage Plants, Elworthy, Lydeard St Lawrence, Taunton, Somerset TA4 3PX ☎ 01984 656 427

Four Seasons Nursery, Forncett St Mary, Norwich, Norfolk NR16 1JT ☎ 01508 488344*

Hoo House Nursery, Gloucester Road, Tewkesbury, Gloucestershire GL20 7DA ☎ 01684 293389

Hillview Hardy Plants, Worfield, Nr Bridgnorth, Shropshire WV15 5NT ☎ 01746 716454 *

Hopleys Plants Ltd, High Street, Much Hadham, Hertfordshire SG10 6BU ☎ 01279 842509 *

Larch Cottage Nurseries, Melkinthorpe, Penrith, Cumbria CA10 2DR ☎ 01931 712404 *

Lingen Nursery, Lingen, Nr Bucknell, Shropshire SY7 0DY ☎ 01544 267720 *

Mill Cottage Plants, The Mill, Henley Lane, Wookey, Somerset BA5 1AP ☎ 01749 676966 *

EUROPE

Bezugsquellen fur Glockenblumen, Gaertnerei Frei, 8461 Wildensbuch, Switzerland.

Staudengaertnerei Sarastro, Christian Kress, 4974 Ort im Innkreis, Austria

Staudengaertnerei Hugin, Zahringstrasse 281, 79108 Freiburg, Germany

F. Sundermann, Alpengarten, 8831 Lindau, Germany

N. AMERICA

SEPI (Seeds and Plants International) 120-3 Marangere, Gatineau, Quebec J8T 6Y9
www3.sympatico.ca

Terra Nova Nurseries, 10051 South Macksburg Rd, Canby, OR 97013, 800-215-3150 ext 21
www.terranovanurseries.com

Other Booklets in the HPS Series

- EPIMEDIUMS AND OTHER HERBACEOUS BERBERIDACEAE

- EUPHORBIAS

- GRASSES

- HARDY GERANIUMS FOR THE GARDEN

- HOSTAS

- PENSTEMONS

- PHLOX

- PULMONARIAS

- SAXIFRAGACEAE - *Some herbaceous members of the Saxifragaceae family*

- UMBELLIFERS

- SUCCESS WITH SEEDS

Apart from *Success with Seeds*, which is a practical guide to collecting, germinating seed and growing on the resultant plants, each booklet provides comprehensive and practical information on garden-worthy plants in its genus. As well as an invaluable A to Z of species and cultivars, the booklets deal with topics such as cultivation, pests and diseases, propagation, and plant associations. Most booklets include appendices giving information on where to see and where to buy the listed plants. The series has been well received and booklets have attracted excellent reviews.